Penguin Modern Poets

————— 10 —————

THE MERSEY SOUND

ADRIAN HENRI

ROGER McGOUGH

BRIAN PATTEN

PENGUIN BOOKS

Penguin Books Ltd, Harmondsworth, Middlesex, England
Penguin Books Inc., 7110 Ambassador Road, Baltimore, Maryland 21207, U.S.A.
Penguin Books Australia Ltd, Ringwood, Victoria, Australia

—

This selection first published 1967
Reprinted 1968 (twice), 1969, 1970 (twice), 1971

—

Copyright © Penguin Books Ltd, 1967

—

Made and printed in Great Britain
by C. Nicholls & Company Ltd
Set in Monotype Garamond

Contents

CONTENTS

ADRIAN HENRI

ADRIAN HENRI

*Tonight at Noon**

(for Charles Mingus and the Clayton Squares)

Tonight at noon
Supermarkets will advertise 3d EXTRA on everything
Tonight at noon
Children from happy families will be sent to live in a home
Elephants will tell each other human jokes
America will declare peace on Russia
World War I generals will sell poppies in the streets on
    November 11th
The first daffodils of autumn will appear
When the leaves fall upwards to the trees

Tonight at noon
Pigeons will hunt cats through city backyards
Hitler will tell us to fight on the beaches and on the landing
    fields
A tunnel full of water will be built under Liverpool
Pigs will be sighted flying in formation over Woolton
and Nelson will not only get his eye back but his arm as well
White Americans will demonstrate for equal rights
in front of the Black House
and the Monster has just created Dr Frankenstein

Girls in bikinis are moonbathing
Folksongs are being sung by real folk
Artgalleries are closed to people over 21
Poets get their poems in the Top 20
Politicians are elected to insane asylums
There's jobs for everyone and nobody wants them
In back alleys everywhere teenage lovers are kissing
in broad daylight

  *The title for this poem is taken from an L.P. by Charles Mingus
'Tonight at Noon', Atlantic 1416.

– 11 –

In forgotten graveyards everywhere the dead will quietly
bury the living
and
You will tell me you love me
Tonight at noon

Adrian Henri's Last Will and Testament

'No one owns life, but anyone who can pick up a fryingpan owns
death.'

William Burroughs

To whom it may concern:

As my imminent death is hourly expected these days/
carbrakes screaming on East Lancs tarmac/trapped
in the blazing cinema/mutely screaming I TOLD YOU SO
from melting eyeballs as the whitehot fireball
dissolves the Cathedral/being the first human being to die
of a hangover/ dying of over-emotion after seeing 20
schoolgirls waiting at a zebracrossing.

I appoint Messrs Bakunin and Kropotkin my executors
and make the following provisions:

1. I leave my priceless collections of Victorian Oil Lamps,
photographs of Hayley Mills, brass fenders and Charlie
Mingus records to all Liverpool poets under 23 who are
also blues singers and failed sociology students.

2. I leave the entire East Lancs Road with all its landscapes
to the British people.

3. I hereby appoint Wm. Burroughs my literary executor,
instructing him to cut up my collected works and
distribute them through the public lavatories of the world.

4. Proceeds from the sale of relics: locks of hair, pieces
of floorboards I have stood on, fragments of bone flesh
teeth bits of old underwear etc. to be given to my widow.

5. I leave my paintings to the Nation with the stipulation
that they must be exhibited in Public Houses,
Chip Shops, Coffee Bars and the Cellar Clubs throughout
the country.

6. Proceeds from the sale of my other effects to be divided
equally amongst the 20 most beautiful schoolgirls in
England (these to be chosen after due deliberation and
exhaustive tests by an informal committee of my friends).

Adrian Henri
Jan. '64

Witnessed this day by:
James Ensor
Charlie 'Bird' Parker.

ADRIAN HENRI

Liverpool Poems

1

GO TO WORK ON A BRAQUE!

2

Youths disguised as stockbrokers
Sitting on the grass eating the Sacred Mushroom.

3

Liverpool I love your horny-handed tons of soil.

4

PRAYER FROM A PAINTER TO ALL CAPITALISTS:
 Open your wallets and repeat after me
  'HELP YOURSELF!'

5

There's one way of being sure of keeping fresh
LIFEBUOY helps you rise again on the 3rd day
after smelling something that smelt like other peoples'
 socks.

6

Note for a definition of optimism:
A man trying the door of Yates Wine Lodge
At quarter past four in the afternoon.

7

I have seen Père UBU walking across Lime St
And Alfred Jarry cycling down Elliott Street.

8

And I saw DEATH in Upper Duke St
Cloak flapping black tall Batman collar
Striding tall shoulders down the hill past the Cathedral
    brown shoes slightly down at the heel

9

Unfrocked Chinese mandarins holding lonely feasts in
    Falkner Sq gardens
to enjoy the snow.

10

Prostitutes in the snow in Canning St like strange erotic
    snowmen
And Marcel Proust in the Kardomah eating Madeleine
    butties dipped in tea.

11

Wyatt James Virgil and Morgan Earp with Doc Holliday
Shooting it out with the Liver Birds at the Pier Head.

12

And a Polish gunman young beautiful dark glasses
combatjacket/staggers down Little St Bride St blood
dripping moaning clutches/collapses down a back jigger
coughing/falls in a wilderness of Dazwhite washing.

Without You

Without you every morning would be like going back to
 work after a holiday,

Without you I couldn't stand the smell of the East Lancs
 Road,

Without you ghost ferries would cross the Mersey manned
 by skeleton crews,

Without you I'd probably feel happy and have more money
 and time and nothing to do with it,

Without you I'd have to leave my stillborn poems on other
 people's doorsteps, wrapped in brown paper,

Without you there'd never be sauce to put on sausage
 butties,

Without you plastic flowers in shop windows wouldjust be
 plastic flowers in shop windows

Without you I'd spend my summers picking morosely over
 the remains of train crashes,

Without you white birds would wrench themselves free
 from my paintings and fly off dripping blood into the
 night,

Without you green apples wouldn't taste greener,

Without you Mothers wouldn't let their children play out
 after tea,

Without you every musician in the world would forget how
 to play the blues,

Without you Public Houses would be public again,

Without you the Sunday Times colour supplement would
 come out in black-and-white,

Without you indifferent colonels would shrug their shoul-
 ders and press the button,

Without you they'd stop changing the flowers in Piccadilly
 Gardens,

Without you Clark Kent would forget how to become
 Superman,

Without you Sunshine Breakfast would only consist of
    Cornflakes,
Without you there'd be no colour in Magic colouring books
Without you Mahler's 8th would only be performed by
    street musicians in derelict houses,
Without you they'd forget to put the salt in every packet of
    crisps,
Without you it would be an offence punishable by a fine of
    up to £200 or two months imprisonment to be found in
    possession of curry powder,
Without you riot police are massing in quiet sidestreets,
Without you all streets would be one-way the other way,
Without you there'd be no one not to kiss goodnight when
    we quarrel,
Without you the first martian to land would turn round and
    go away again,
Without you they'd forget to change the weather,
Without you blind men would sell unlucky heather,
Without you there would be
no landscapes/no stations/no houses,
no chipshops/no quiet villages/no seagulls
on beaches/no hopscotch on pavements/no
night/no morning/there'd be no city no country
Without you.

Love Is ...

Love is feeling cold in the back of vans
Love is a fanclub with only two fans
Love is walking holding paintstained hands
Love is

Love is fish and chips on winter nights
Love is blankets full of strange delights
Love is when you don't put out the light
Love is

Love is the presents in Christmas shops
Love is when you're feeling Top of the Pops
Love is what happens when the music stops
Love is

Love is white panties lying all forlorn
Love is a pink nightdress still slightly warm
Love is when you have to leave at dawn
Love is

Love is you and love is me
Love is a prison and love is free
Love's what's there when you're away from me
Love is ...

Morning Poem

(for Deirdre)

'I've just about reached
breaking point'
he snapped.

Drinking Song

He became more and more drunk
As the afternoon wore off.

Song for a Beautiful Girl Petrol-pump Attendant on the Motorway

I wanted your soft verges
But you gave me the hard shoulder.

Poem for Roger McGough

A nun in a supermarket
standing in the queue
Wondering what its like
To buy groceries for two.

Song of Affluence or I Wouldn't Leave My 8-Roomed House for You

I wouldn't leave my little 8-roomed house for you
I've got one missus and I don't want two

I love you baby but you must understand
That feeling you's fine and kissing you's grand
But I wouldn't leave my little wooden wife for you

Water tastes fine but money tastes sweeter
I'd rather have a fire than a paraffin heater
And
I wouldn't change my little 8-roomed life for you.

Love Poem/Colour Supplement

It was our first great war
And after the first successful sortie
Into the nomansgland
between her thighs
We waited anxiously every month
for poppysellers to appear in her streets

On the Late Late Massachers Stillbirths and Deformed Children a Smoother Lovelier Skin Job

The seven-day beauty plan:
Avenge O Lord thy slaughter'd saints, whose bones
Will cause up to 1 million deaths from leukaemia
Forget not, in thy book record their groans
Now for the vitally important step. Cream your face and
    neck a second time
No American president world-famous for beauty creams
responsible for the freedom and safety of so many young
    offenders
TODAY'S MEN OF ACTION
The Triple Tyrant Macmillan Kennedy Watkinson
The West governments are satisfied as to the moral
    necessity to resume Racing from Newmarket
EXTRA SPECIAL!
Atmospheric testing: A test card is shown
continuously from 10 a.m. until 15 minutes
before slayn by the bloody Piemontese
why pay higher fares?
There is always trouble when President Kennedy the jovial
    gravel-voiced little sailor
defends glamorous Olive Oyl from contamination of the
    atmosphere
EXTRA MONEY their moans
The Vales redoubled to the Hills
Another fire blazes in the city of London AND ALL THAT
    JAZZ
Do you draw your curtains with a walking-stick?
The mutation was caused by a heavy dose of radiation
    received
by the Mother at Hiroshima
This baby's eyes and nose had merged into

one misshapen feature in the middle of its
forehead lost 6″ from Hips
sufferers can now wear fashion stockings
Early may fly the Babylonian wo
followed by
TOMORROW'S WEATHER
The Epilogue
close down.

Cut-up of John Milton Sonnet XV On the late
Massacher in Piemont/TV Times/CND leaflet.

Great War Poems

1. The same old soldiers walking along the same old skyline

2. Dead hand through the sandbags reaching out for the cream-and-white butterfly

3. mud/water under duckboards/mud/rats scamper in starshell darkness/mud/smell of shit and rotting bodies/mud/resting your sweaty forehead on the sandbags OVER THE TOP the first men in the lunar landscape.

4. 'What did you do to the Great Whore, Daddy?'

5. Poppies slightly out-of-focus and farmcarts bringing in the peaceful dead.

6. The ghost of Wilfred Owen selling matches outside the Burlington Arcade.

7. Seafog. Red flaring lights from the shorebatteries. The roar of shells rattle of machineguns. Water running in the bilges. My feet slipping on the damp cobbles of the quayside.

8. DON'T BE VAGUE — BLAME GENERAL HAIG.

9. four white feathers clutched in a blood-stained envelope

10. a skull nestling in a bed of wild strawberries/boots mouldering green with fungus/saplings thrusting through rusting helmets/sunken barges drifting full of leaves down autumn rivers.

Country Song

'Lily of the Valley (Convalaria Majalis, fam. Lilliaceae). Grows wild in N. England. Commonly cultivated. Flowers in May. Berries red when ripe. Leaves particularly poisonous because three constituents depress the heart, like Foxglove.'

What are the constituents that depress the heart?
the scent of lilies in darkgreen silences under trees
milkweed and ragwort and sunshine in hedges
small flowers picked amongst trees when it's raining

A year ago
You planted lilies in the valley of my mind
There were lilies at the bottom of my garden
And ferrys at the bottom of my street

Now
I sit here in sunlight with the smell of wild garlic
Trying to taperecord the sound of windflowers and
    celandines

Wondering
What are the three constituents that depress the heart
Without you here in the country?

Holcombe Poem/Poem For a Girl I Didn't Meet

walking on the moors thinking about how I didn't meet
    you yesterday
heather underfoot and mist over Pendle
the moor changing like an animal/brown to green grey to
    purple with the weather
sky blue at the edges
                        like a letter that came too late.

... *Undine rising from the waters her golden hair*
dripping in the moonlight ... dead bird on a fence blood
dripping from its neck ... Isis searching the rushes
for her murdered lover ... small girl with a fishingrod
in a rushing valley full of ferns ... the last supper
followed by the Four Just Desserts ... watching the
white mocking figure at the edge of the Dark Forest
... beating naked blondhaired girls with
longstemmed purple flowers ... Osiris judging
the dead mist rising up the valley seaweed tangled
in her moonlight hair ...

trains
    moving through valleys
chimneys
    springing from hillsides
streams
    tumbling through boulders
clouds
    tilting from the horizon
and
    me
    on the moors
thinking about the girl I never met.

Me

if you weren't you, who would you like to be?

Paul McCartney Gustav Mahler
Alfred Jarry John Coltrane
Charlie Mingus Claude Debussy
Wordsworth Monet Bach and Blake

Charlie Parker Pierre Bonnard
Leonardo Bessie Smith
Fidel Castro Jackson Pollock
Gaudi Milton Munch and Berg

Belà Bartók Henri Rousseau
Rauschenberg and Jasper Johns
Lukas Cranach Shostakovich
Kropotkin Ringo George and John

William Burroughs Francis Bacon
Dylan Thomas Luther King
H. P. Lovecraft T. S. Eliot
D. H. Lawrence Roland Kirk

Salvatore Giuliano
Andy Warhol Paul Cézanne
Kafka Camus Ensor Rothko
Jacques Prévert and Manfred Mann

Marx Dostoevsky
Bakunin Ray Bradbury
Miles Davis Trotsky
Stravinsky and Poe

Danilo Dolci Napoleon Solo
St John of the Cross and
The Marquis de Sade

Charles Rennie Mackintosh
Rimbaud Claes Oldenburg
Adrian Mitchell and Marcel Duchamp

James Joyce and Hemingway
Hitchcock and Buñuel
Donald McKinlay Thelonius Monk

Alfred, Lord Tennyson
Matthias Grünewald
Philip Jones Griffiths and Roger McGough

Guillaume Apollinaire
Cannonball Adderley
René Magritte
Hieronymus Bosch

Stéphane Mallarmé and Alfred de Vigny
Ernst Mayakovsky and Nicolas de Staël
Hindemith Mick Jagger Dürer and Schwitters
Garcia Lorca
        and
            last of all
                me.

Hello Adrian

(for Adrian Mitchell)

Hello Adrian,

   This is me, Adrian. I hope you had a nice Christmas as it finds us here. We had that nice Mr and Mrs Johnson to tea who's president of something but they didn't like those yellow people from across the road. Christmas had us a bit worried but Santaclaus in his big Red Cloak came down her chimney and now all those cards with cribs on won't be in bad taste after all. Very strange things have been happening lately. People keep falling off cliffs and into bed with me. Last night I met Paul McCartney in a suburban garden wearing a moustache drawn by Marcel Duchamp. I keep wanting to sign shelves of tins in Supermarkets. Everytime I go for coal the coalplace is full of dead Vietcong. Birds have eaten the berries off our plastic holly. I think it's going to be a hard winter.

   Today is New Year's Day, should Auld Acquaintance be Forgot? I don't know but my stomach feels funny. I have sent messages to the leaders of the various parts of my body asking them to end the fighting NOW. There's no shillings left in the meter we'll have to roast a leg of pork over the gasfire. Someone's left the front door open O My God we might have had thieves murderers nutters queers anyone coming up here. Now someones taken the cat and left a shovel instead.

   People keep offering me nebulous schemes for making my fortune in various of The Arts. A girl told me 'I had a dreadful time on Christmas Day, Uncle Gerald kept putting his hand up my skirt'. There were huge punch-ups in Woolworths on Christmas Eve. I have seen the entire Works of Charles Dickens on the telly this Christmas ... Oliver Twist going to see Miss Havisham with Tiny Tim ... Scrooge skating with Mr Pickwick ... Pip stealing handkerchiefs to give to Little Nell ... I can't stand it any longer if those Chuzzlewits call again we're *definitely* not at home. I'm making New Year Resolutions again but I'm not likely to meet her *this* year either. I'm going to have my poems on Cash's Woven Nametapes put inside schoolgirls' gymslips. I'm going to treat white Rhodesians as equals. I've forgotten all the others already.

I think Spring must be coming. She brought me a bunch of plastic violets yesterday. I can hear the noise of the ice-floes breaking up on the bathroom floor. There's still no one waiting by the waterfall: I looked again today.

I really must close now as the Last Post is sounding, so hoping this finds you as it leaves me love to all at No. 18 from all at No. 64.

Adrian

Adrian Henri's Talking After Christmas Blues

Well I woke up this mornin' it was Christmas Day
And the birds were singing the night away
I saw my stocking lying on the chair
Looked right to the bottom but you weren't there
there was

>   apples
>   oranges
>   chocolates
>   .... aftershave

– but no you.

So I went downstairs and the dinner was fine
There was pudding and turkey and lots of wine
And I pulled those crackers with a laughing face
Till I saw there was no one in your place
there was

>   mincepies
>   brandy
>   nuts and raisins
>   .... mashed potato

– but no you.

Now it's New Year and it's Auld Lang Syne
And it's 12 o'clock and I'm feeling fine
Should Auld Acquaintance be Forgot?
I don't know girl, but it hurts a lot
there was

>   whisky
>   vodka
>   dry Martini (stirred
>   but not shaken)

.... and 12 New Year resolutions
– all of them about you.

So it's all the best for the year ahead
As I stagger upstairs and into bed
Then I looked at the pillow by my side
....I tell you baby I almost cried
there'll be

> Autumn
>> Summer
>>> Spring
>>>> ....and Winter

– all of them without you.

The Blazing Hat, Part Two

This is the morning that we burnt a cardboard hat
flames licking the inside of the brim
This is the morning that the thunder hung like great
  black flags over the city
stirred by gusts of wind
This is the morning that they opened a new motorway
leading from my house to yours
This is the morning that I decided I wasn't getting enough
  roughage
and went on a diet of broken milkbottles
This is the morning that Death left her cloak behind
after the party
This is the morning that a beautiful schoolgirl woke me
  with a cup of coffee
in a vision
This is the morning that we saw
words written on water
This is the morning that beautiful girls with Renaissance
  faces played Hindemith records
at dawn
This is the morning after the night
before
This is the morning after the night
had strewn Canning Street with purple toiletrolls
This is the morning that we saw a 4-year-old boy
whipping an imaginary blonde lovely
This is the morning that Death was a letter
that was never scented
This is the morning that the poet reached out for the
  rolled-up Financial Times
followed by a dreadful explosion
This is the morning that you woke up 50 miles away
  seeing sunlight on the water

and didn't think of me
This is the morning that I bought 16 different kinds of
    artificial lilies-of-the-valley
all of them smelling of you
This is the morning that we sat and talked
by the embers of the blazing hat.

Pictures From an Exhibition

(Painting and Sculpture of a Decade 54–64 Tate Gallery London
April–June 1964)

No. 54 Jean Dubuffet 'Déclinaison de la Barbe' 1· 1959
' as-tu cueilli les fleurs de la barbe?'
Jean Dubuffet I wander the dark pebbles of your mind
picking beardflowers.

No. 73 Joseph Cornell 'Hôtel de l 'Étoile'
cool pillars of the hotel/in the
night outside the stars are always
so white/the sky is always so
blue/silver moon waiting patiently.

No. 84 Mark Rothko 'Reds - No. 22' 1957
SCARLET
ORANGE
ORANGE
ORANGE
SCARLET
CRIMSON
SCARLET

No. 291 Robert Rauschenberg 'Windward' 1963
printed oranges are painted
painted oranges are painted

Angry skyline over the gasworks
A Hawk sits brooding inside a painted rainbow.

Nos. 10-13 Josef Albers, Studies for 'Homage to the Square' 1961-2

look.

see.

long ago.

now.

No. 314 Bernard Requichot 'Sans Titre - Chasse de papiers choisis'

chasse aux papillons:
'Here Be Tygers' –
– the fruit in the tin has a thousand eyes.

No. 349 Jim Dine 'Black Bathroom No. 2' 1962

black splashes on the white walls
interrupting the commercials
TURN ON THE GLEAMING WHITE SINK
AND POEMS COME OUT OF THE TAPS!

No. 139 Victor Vasarely 'Supernovae' 1959-61

BLACK IS WHITE
BLACK IS WHITE
WHITE IS BLACK
WHITE IS BLACK

No. 50 Louise Nevelson 'Sky Cathedral III' 1960

Black
> Black

Black
> Boxes

Black
> Light

Black
> Moonlight

Black
> Emptiness

Black
> Dust

Black
> Boxes

Black
> Black

Black

No. 247 Richard Diebenkorn 'Ingleside' 1963

Look through the Supermarket window/up the highway
the hill rises steeply/hoardings and magnolias bright
in the sunlight/white walls black freeways trafficsigns
at intersections/green lawns dark hedges/colours
clear and bright as the packets in your wire basket.

Love Poem

(Sections from a work still in progress)

East Lancs
Road Poems
Snow scattering on the windscreen/blowing
from the drystone moors/I think of you.

My central nervous system has gone: my
ganglia aren't even on the AA map. My
       heart is
single-line traffic, one way only.

London Poems
On the tube after seeing Rauschenberg
the tube a huge construction where he had
       cunningly
       got people reflected in the windows and
       posters moving past

You and Père Ubu holding hands in Piccadilly
Walking off into the COCA COLA sunset

'Heather
Holden, 16,
Haslingden
Grammar
School
"Haslingden
Moors with
Snow"'
Beautiful/Hair falling over eyes/hands cold
       holding sketchbook/
crowded noisy schoolroom/postercolours/tiny
       blue uniform
frozen at the corner of a field/waiting to meet
       her first lover after school

Hate Poem
'To know know know you
Is to love love love you'
And I don't.

Love Poem
ANY RECORD IN THE TOP 20 ANYTIME
    IS OUR TUNE

An empty Colgate tube
An almond with ALMOND written on it
breakfastpink gingham shirt & red waistcoat like
    tomatoes
a bar of rock lettered all through with your name
    and a plastic flower
a pair of your old navyblue schooldrawers
an empty Drambuie bottle & an empty packet of
    export cigarettes
a signed copy of this poem
a chocolate Easter Egg
A photograph:
Little smiling girl in bra and knickers sitting
in a summer field
A red bra with I LOVE YOU written inside one of
    the cups
A painting of a shocking pink heart with your name
    scratched on it
Some rusting scissors and a decaying fan from a dead
    King's treasurehouse.

Assemblage of Objects and Mementoes

'Bluetit Patrol 2nd 15th Rossendale Girl Guides' Summer Camp Arnside 1960'

Our love is watched over by all my masters;
Picabia watches from his cacodynamic eye
Max Ernst looks on as impersonally as when he
    watched
the Virgin Mary spanking the infant Jesus
Guillaume Apollinaire in Piccadilly Bus Station
watches the unlikely couple walking the cold
    streets
Monk takes his hands off the keyboard and smiles
    approvingly
The Beatles sing lullabys for our never-to-happen
    children
Quietly in the shadows by Central Station

Manchester Poem

William Burroughs sits dunking Pound Cake in coffee
        waiting for the last connection
and sees us through the window
Bartók has orchestrated the noise of the tulips in
        Piccadilly Gardens for us
Marcel Duchamp has added your photograph to
        the Green Box
Dylan Thomas staggers into the Cromwell for one
        last one
and waves across to us
Kurt Schwitters smiles as he picks up the two pink
        bus tickets
we have just thrown away
Parker blows another chorus of Loverman for us
Ensor smiles behind his mask
Jarry cycles slowly behind us down Spring Gardens

Rauschenberg and Jasper Johns
Bless the bed we lie upon

Lakeland   Daffodils grow in the shadows of your hair
Poem   Waterfalls in the hollows of your throat
                Your body a bright lake seen between houses
                        catching the morning sun
                Pale lilies-of-the-valley in the darkness of your thighs

Boots   I've had 3 new prs. of boots since I met you
                And I keep thinking perhaps I should get a
                        new relationship as well
                But I don't need to:
                Perhaps it's the kind that doesn't wear out.

Lawn   I think of you
                Even when walking with beautiful girls
                On the lawn of rich men's houses at night

Where the sky is mowed every morning
And the stars are switched on when the guests arrive

Wind blowing inland from the Pierhead
I was glad to be seen with you in Liverpool
Dead ferryboats in the shadows between your hair
    and cheek.

*Liverpool
Poem*

Wild West Poems

1. Noon:
    2 tall gunmen walking slowly towards each other down
    Mathew St.

2. '*And then he grabbed her*   (for Leiber/Stoller
    And then   and the Coasters)
            He tied her up
    And then
            He lit the fuse to the dynamite
    And then
    And then
    AND THEN
            ALONG CAME JONES ...'

3. William H. Bonney alias Billy the Kid hitches his horse
    to a parkingmeter strides through the swing doors into
    Yates Wine Lodge. Barmaids slowly back away from the
    counter. Drunks rush out into Charlotte Street. He
    drinks a glass of Aussie White and strides out, silent as
    he came.

4. POEM FOR BLACK BART TO LEAVE BEHIND ON A
    STAGECOACH
    I hope you ladies ain't afraid
    Of the wicked man who made this raid
    But I'm like nature quick and cruel
    Believe me, gals, I need them jewels.

5. The Daltons riding down Church Street/Bullets
    ricochet off streetsigns/windows full of cardboard
    Walkers bottles shatter/Bob Grat Emmett
    thunder across trafficlights at red/hoofbeats
    die away clattering down Lord Street.

Poem in Memoriam T. S. Eliot

I'd been out the night before & hadn't seen the papers or
    the telly
& the next day in a café someone told me you were dead
And it was as if a favourite distant uncle had died
old hands in the bigstrange room/new shiny presents at
    Christmas
and I didn't know what to feel.

For years I measured out my life with your coffeespoons

Your poems on the table in dusty bedsitters
Playing an L.P. of you reading on wet interrupted January
    afternoons

Meanwhile, back at the Wasteland:
Maureen O'Hara in a lowcut dress staggers across Rhyl
    sandhills
Lovers in Liverpool pubs eating passionfruit
Reading Alfred de Vigny in the lavatory
Opening an old grand piano and finding it smelling of
    curry
THE STAR OF INDIA FOUND IN A BUS STATION
Making love in a darkened room hearing an old woman
    having a fit on the landing
The first snowflakes of winter falling on her Christmas
    poem for me in Piccadilly Gardens
The first signs of spring in plastic daffodils
on city counters

Lovers kissing
Rain falling

Dogs running
Night falling

And you 'familiar compound spirit' moving silently down
   Canning St in a night of rain and fog.

ADRIAN HENRI

Where'er You Walk

'Where'er you walk
Cool gales shall fan that glade'

The Pierhead where you walked will be made a park
restricted to lovers under 21
Peasants will be found merrymaking after the storm in
    Canning St
where you walked
The station where we first arrived at night
Will be preserved for the nation
With the echo of your footsteps still sounding in the empty
    roof

'Where'er you tread
The Blushing flower shall rise'

The alleyway where we read poems to dustbins
after closing time
The kitchens where we quarrelled at parties
The kitchen where two strangers first kissed at a party
full of strangers
The ticketbarrier where we said goodnight so many times
The cobblestones in front of the station
The pub where the kindly old waiter
Always knows what we want to drink —
ALL SHALL BURST INTO BLOOM
SPROUTING FLOWERS BRIGHTER THAN PLASTIC ONES
    IN WOOLWORTHS
Daffodils and chrysanthemums, rhododendrons and
    snowdrops, tulips and roses
— cobblestones bursting with lilies-of-the-valley

'And all things flourish'

Whole streets where you walk are paved with soft grass
so the rain will never go through your shoes again
Zebracrossings made of lilies
Belishabeacons made of orangeblossom
Busstops huge irises
Trafficlights made of snapdragons

'Trees where you sit
Shall crowd into a shade'

even in Piccadilly
stations covered in flowers yellow like the paint you once
    got in your hair
Oaktrees growing everywhere we've kissed
Will still be there when I've forgotten what you look like
And you don't remember me at all
Copies of your letters to me on blue paper
Written on the sky by an aeroplane over all the cities of
    england
Copies of your poems stamped on eggs instead of lions
We will walk forever in the darkness under fernleaves

'Trees where you sit
shall crowd into a shade'

ADRIAN HENRI

The New 'Our Times'

(for Félix Fénéon)*

I

At 3 p.m. yesterday, a Mr Adolphus Edwards, a Jamaican immigrant, was pecked to death by a large Bronze Eagle in Upper Parliament St. A U.S. State Dept. spokesman said later, 'We have no comment to make as of this time.'

2

Police-Constable George Williams, who was partially blinded by a 15 lb. jellybaby thrown at a passing pop singer, is to be retired on half-pension.

3

Bearded Liverpool couple put out of misery in night by drip oil heater, court told.

4

A certain Mrs Elspeth Clout, of Huyton, was killed by an unidentified falling object. It was thought to be a particularly hard stool evacuated from the toilet of a passing aeroplane.

5

2 chip-shop proprietors were today accused of selling human ears fried in batter. One of them said 'We believe there is room for innovation in the trade.'

6

Fatality in Kardomah bomb outrage: Waitress buried Alive under two thousand Danish pastries.

*(a free 1960s Liverpool version of Fénéon's great 'Our Times'.)

7

At the inquest on Paul McCartney, aged 21, described as a
popular singer and guitarist, P.C. Smith said, in evidence,
that he saw one of the accused, Miss Jones, standing waving
bloodstained hands shouting 'I got a bit of his liver.'

In the Midnight Hour

When we meet
in the midnight hour
country girl
I will bring you nightflowers
coloured like your eyes
in the moonlight
in the midnight
hour

I remember

Your cold hand
held for a moment among strangers
held for a moment among dripping trees
in the midnight hour

I remember

Your eyes coloured like the autumn landscape
walking down muddy lanes
watching sheep eating yellow roses
walking in city squares in winter rain
kissing in darkened hallways
walking in empty suburban streets
saying goodnight in deserted alleyways

in the midnight hour

Andy Williams singing 'We'll keep a Welcome in the
    Hillsides' for us
When I meet you at the station
The Beatles singing 'We Can Work it Out' with James
    Ensor at the harmonium
Rita Hayworth in a nightclub singing 'Amade Mia'

I will send you armadas
of love vast argosies of flowers
in the midnight hour
country girl

when we meet

in the
moonlight
midnight
hour
country girl

I will bring you

yellow
white
eyes
bright
moon
light
mid
night
flowers
in the midnight hour.

I Want To Paint

PART ONE

I want to paint
2000 dead birds crucified on a background of night
Thoughts that lie too deep for tears
Thoughts that lie too deep for queers
Thoughts that move at 186000 miles/second
The Entry of Christ into Liverpool in 1966
The Installation of Roger McGough to the Chair of Poetry
    at Oxford
Francis Bacon making the President's Speech at the Royal
    Academy Dinner

I want to paint
50 life-sized nudes of Marianne Faithfull
(all of them painted from life)
Welsh Maids by Welsh Waterfalls
Heather Holden as Our Lady of Haslingden
A painting as big as Piccadilly full of neon signs buses
Christmas decorations and beautiful girls with dark blonde
    hair shading their faces

I want to paint
The assassination of the entire Royal Family
Enormous pictures of every pavingstone in Canning Street
The Beatles composing a new National Anthem
Brian Patten writing poems with a flamethrower on disused
    ferryboats

A new cathedral 50 miles high made entirely of pram-
    wheels
An empty Woodbine packet covered in kisses
I want to paint
A picture made from the tears of dirty-faced children in
    Chatham Street

I want to paint
I LOVE YOU across the steps of St George's Hall
I want to paint
                    pictures.

PART TWO

I want to paint
The Simultaneous and Historical Faces of Death
10000 shocking pink hearts with your name on
The phantom negro postmen who bring me money in my
    dreams
The first plastic daffodil of Spring pushing its way
through the OMO packets in the Supermarket
The portrait of every 6th Form schoolgirl in the country
A full-scale map of the World with YOU at the centre
An enormous lily-of-the-valley with every flower on a
    separate canvas

Lifesize jellybabies shaped like Hayley Mills
A black-and-red flag flying over Parliament
I want to paint
Every car crash on all the motorways of England
Père Ubu drunk at 11 o'clock at night in Lime Street
A SYSTEMATIC DERANGEMENT OF ALL THE SENSES
In black running letters 50 miles high over Liverpool

I want to paint
Pictures that children can play hopscotch on
Pictures that can be used as evidence at Murder trials
Pictures that can be used to advertise cornflakes
Pictures that can be used to frighten naughty children
Pictures worth their weight in money
Pictures that tramps can live in
Pictures that children would find in their stockings on
    Christmas morning
Pictures that teenage lovers can send each other
I want to paint
                    pictures.

ADRIAN HENRI

Don't Worry/Everything's Going to be All Right

Don't worry
If your boyfriend doesn't treat you right
baby
Everything's going to be all right
come with me
And every poem I write will have your name in it
Don't worry
If the factories and villas cover the countryside
Everything's going to be all right
England will be given back to the animals
and we'll find a home under fernleaves known only to foxes
Don't worry
If I can't afford to buy you coffee after school
Everything's going to be all right
Soon the poem will replace the pound sterling as
    international currency
and Britain will get on the poem standard again
Don't worry
About those lunatics in the government
Everything's going to be all right
The country will be governed by beautiful girls under 18
(and you will let me carry your portfolio home from the
    House)
Don't worry
About what happened the other night
Everything's going to be all right
They'll give you contraceptive pills shaped like jellybabies
    with your milk at playtime
Don't worry
about what your Dad says about the younger generation
Everything's going to be all right
There'll be involuntary euthanasia for everyone over 30
not a poet painter or musician

Don't worry
About the rain
Everything's going to be all right
The streets will be covered with tiny pink flowers
like the ones on your suspenderbelt
Bathingsuits will be banned from beaches
School uniforms will be the only kind allowed in public
Your end-of-term report will be marked out of 100 for sex
    appeal
(and you will be Top of the Form)
Policemen will be beaten up by poets
Trade Unions will be taken over by workers
There'll be 24-hour licensing
And everything will be on the National Drink Service
your parents will wake us every morning with breakfast
Your teacher will smile at notes saying we stayed in bed late
Your face will be in every art gallery
Your name in every book of poetry
So
Don't worry
Everything's going to be all right.

Mrs Albion You've Got a Lovely Daughter
(for Allen Ginsberg)

Albion's most lovely daughter sat on the banks of the
   Mersey dangling her landing stage in the water.

The daughters of Albion
   arriving by underground at Central Station
   eating hot ecclescakes at the Pierhead
   writing 'Billy Blake is fab' on a wall in Mathew St

   taking off their navyblue schooldrawers and
   putting on nylon panties ready for the night

The daughters of Albion
   see the moonlight beating down on them in Bebington
   throw away their chewinggum ready for the goodnight
     kiss
sleep in the dinnertime sunlight with old men
   looking up their skirts in St Johns Gardens
comb their darkblonde hair in suburban bedrooms
powder their delicate little nipples/wondering if tonight
    will be the night
their bodies pressed into dresses or sweaters
lavender at The Cavern or pink at The Sink

The daughters of Albion
   wondering how to explain why they didn't go home

The daughters of Albion
   taking the dawn ferry to tomorrow
   worrying about what happened
   worrying about what hasn't happened
   lacing up blue sneakers over brown ankles
   fastening up brown stockings to blue suspenderbelts

Beautiful boys with bright red guitars
in the spaces between the stars

Reelin' an' a-rockin'
Wishin' an' a-hopin'
Kissin' an' a-prayin'
Lovin' an' a-layin'

Mrs Albion you've got a lovely daughter.

ROGER McGOUGH

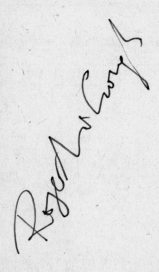

Comeclose and Sleepnow

it is afterwards
and you talk on tiptoe
happy to be part
of the darkness
lips becoming limp
a prelude to tiredness.
Comeclose and Sleepnow
for in the morning
when a policeman
disguised as the sun
creeps into the room
and your mother
disguised as birds
calls from the trees
you will put on a dress of guilt
and shoes with broken high ideals
and refusing coffee
run
alltheway
home.

Aren't We All

Looks quite pretty lying there
Can't be asleep yet
Wonder what she's thinking about?
Penny for her thoughts
Probably not worth it.
There's the moon trying to look romantic
Moon's too old that's her trouble
Aren't we all?

Lace curtains gently swaying
Like a woman walking
A woman ina negligee
Walking out through the window
Over the sleeping city up into the sky
To give the moon a rest
Moon's too tired that's her trouble
Aren't we all?

Wasn't a bad party really
Except for the people
People always spoil things
Room's in a mess
And this one's left her clothes allover the place
Scattered like seeds
In too much of a hurry that's her trouble
Aren't we all?

Think she's asleep now
It makes you sleep
Better than Horlicks
Not so pretty really when you get close-up
Wonder what her name is?
Now she's taken all the blankets
Too selfish that's her trouble
Aren't we all?

A lot of Water has Flown under your Bridge

i remember your hands
white and strangely cold
asif exposed too often to the moon

i remember your eyes
brown and strangely old
asif exposed too often and too soon

i remember your body
young and strangely bold
asif exposed too often

i remember
i remember how
when you laughed
hotdogmen allover town
burst into song

i remember
i remember how
when you cried
the clouds cried too and the
streets became awash with tears

i remember
i remember how
when we lay together for the first time
the room smiled,
said: 'excuse-me',
and tiptoed away.

but time has passed since then
and alotof people
have crossed over the bridge
(a faceless throng)

but time has passed since then
and alotof youngmen
have swum in the water
(naked and strong)

but time has passed since then
and alotof water
   has flown
     under
      your
        bridge.

ROGER McGOUGH

On Picnics

at the goingdown of the sun
and in the morning
i try to remember them
but their names are ordinary names
and their causes are thighbones
tugged excitedly from the soil
by frenchchildren
on picnics

Café Portraits

A lonelylady with perfumed hair
is eating primly and with care
lest she should drop a bean
onto her clean suitable skirt
and ruin the illusion
of sophistication.

A pair of pensioners nibble
at their cups of tea
their mouths saying oldfashioned things
(for their minds are many miles ago)
one twirling the sugarbowl
with boney fingers
the other drawing daydreams
in the spilt milk.

A blueeyed girl
is sitting waiting
beautifully with
legs crossed easily
for her lightfingered leatherthighed lover
who will say things as sweet as icing
and carry her off between the cruets
to his castle on the hill.
And dreaming of the pleasures there
with littlefinger in the air
she ravishes her third eclair.

A thinman
with a pubic smile
eating herringroes
with neat copperplate movements
dreams of choristers – on toast.

Two portly menopausing women
with varicosemarbled legs and
Danish pastries
speak justso ideas agreeably
and longfor presanitary days
when they sucked pigs' eggs
and played ollies in the
knockeruppered barefooted tripe and fishcaked streets.

The Fallen Birdman

The oldman in the cripplechair
Died in transit through the air
And slopped into the road.

The driver of the lethallorry
Trembled out and cried: 'I'm sorry,
But it was his own fault'.

Humans snuggled round the mess
In masochistic tenderness
As raindrops danced in his womb.

. . . . . .

But something else obsessed my brain,
The canvas, twistedsteel and cane,
His chair, spreadeagled in the rain,
Like a fallen birdman.

The Icingbus

the littleman
with the hunchbackedback
creptto his feet
to offer his seat
to the blindlady

people gettingoff
steered carefully around
the black mound
of his back
as they would a pregnantbelly

the littleman
completely unaware
of the embarrassment behind
watched as the blindlady
fingered out her fare

. . . . . .

muchlove later he suggested that instead
ofa wedding-cake they shouldhave a miniaturebus
made outof icing but she laughed
andsaid that buses werefor travelling in
and notfor eating and besides
you cant taste shapes.

You and Your Strange Ways

increasingly oftennow
you reach into your handbag
(the one I bought some xmasses ago)
and bringing forth
a pair of dead cats
skinned and glistening
like the undersides of tongues
or old elastoplasts
sticky with earwigs
you hurl them at my eyes
and laugh cruellongly
why?
even though we have grown older together
and my kisses are little more than functional
i still love you
you and your strange ways

At Lunchtime   A Story of Love

When the busstopped suddenly to avoid
damaging a mother and child in the road, the
younglady in the greenhat sitting opposite
was thrown across me, and not being one to
miss an opportunity i started to makelove
with all my body.

At first she resisted saying that it
was tooearly in the morning and toosoon
after breakfast and that anyway she found
me repulsive. But when i explained that
this being a nuclearage, the world was going
to end at lunchtime, she tookoff her
greenhat, put her busticket in her pocket
and joined in the exercise.

The buspeople, and therewere many of
them, were shockedandsurprised and amused-
andannoyed, but when the word got around
that the world was coming to an end at lunch-
time, they put their pride in their pockets
with their bustickets and madelove one with
the other. And even the busconductor, being
over, climbed into the cab and struck up
some sort of relationship with the driver.

Thatnight, on the bus coming home,
wewere all alittle embarrassed, especially me
and the younglady in the greenhat, and we
all started to say in different ways howhasty
and foolish we had been. Butthen, always
having been a bitofalad, i stood up and
said it was a pity that the world didn't nearly

end every lunchtime and that we could always
pretend. And then it happened ...

Quick asa crash we all changed partners
and soon the bus was aquiver with white
mothballbodies doing naughty things.

> And the next day
> And everyday
> In everybus
> In everystreet
> In everytown
> In everycountry

people pretended that the world was coming
to an end at lunchtime. It still hasn't.
Although in a way it has.

Icarus Allsorts

*'A meteorite is reported to have landed
in New England. No damage is said ...'*

A littlebit of heaven fell
From out the sky one day
It landed in the ocean
Not so very far away
The General at the radar screen
Rubbed his hands with glee
And grinning pressed the button
That started World War Three.

From every corner of the earth
Bombs began to fly
There were even missile jams
No traffic lights in the sky
In the times it takes to blow your nose
The people fell, the mushrooms rose

'House!' cried the fatlady
As the bingohall moved to various parts
of the town

'Raus!' cried the German butcher
as his shop came tumbling down

Philip was in the countinghouse
Counting out his money
The Queen was in the parlour
Eating bread and honey
When through the window
Flew a bomb
And made them go all funny

(By the way if you're wondering
What happened to the maid
Well in this particular raid
She lost more than her nose
In fact she came to a close
Or so the story goes.)

In the time it takes to draw a breath
Or eat a toadstool, instant death.

The rich
Huddled outside the doors of their fallout shelters
Like drunken carolsingers

The poor
Clutching shattered televisions
And last week's editions of T.V. Times
(but the very last)

Civil defence volunteers
Withtheir tin hats in one hand
And their heads in the other

CND supporters
Their ban the bomb mojos beginning to rust
Have scrawled 'I told you so' in the dust.

A littlebit of heaven fell
From out the sky one day
It landed in Vermont
North-Eastern U.S.A.
The general at the radar screen
He should have got the sack
But that wouldn't bring
Three thousand million, seven hundred,
    and sixty-eight people back,
Would it?

Why Patriots are a Bit Nuts in the Head

Patriots are a bit nuts in the head
because they wear
red, white and blue-
tinted spectacles
(red for blood
white for glory
and blue ...
for a boy)
and are in effervescent danger
of losing their lives
lives are good for you
when you are alive
you can eat and drink a lot
and go out with girls
(sometimes if you are lucky
   you can even go to bed with them)
but you can't do this
if you have your belly shot away
and your seeds
spread over some corner of a foreign field
to facilitate
in later years
the growing of oats by some peasant yobbo

when you are posthumous it is cold and dark
and that is why patriots are a bit nuts in the head

Sad Aunt Madge

As the cold winter evenings drew near
Aunt Madge used to put extra blankets
over the furniture, to keep it warm and cosy.
Mussolini was her lover, and life
was an outoffocus rosy-tinted spectacle.

but neurological experts
with kind blueeyes
and gentle voices
small white hands
and large Rolls Royces
said that electric shock treatment
should do the trick
it did . . .

today after 15 years of therapeutic tears
and an awful lot of ratepayers' shillings
down the hospital meter
sad Aunt Madge
no longer tucks up the furniture
before kissing it goodnight
and admits
that her affair with Mussolini
clearly was not right
particularly in the light
of her recently announced engagement
to the late pope.

My Busconductor

My busconductor tells me
he only has one kidney
and that may soon go on strike
through overwork.
Each busticket
takes on now a different shape
and texture.
He holds a ninepenny single
as if it were a rose
and puts the shilling in his bag
as a child into a gasmeter.
His thin lips
have no quips
for fat factorygirls
and he ignores
the drunk who snores
and the oldman who talks to himself
and gets off at the wrong stop.
He goes gently to the bedroom
of the bus
to collect
and watch familiar shops and pubs passby
(perhaps for the last time?)
The sameold streets look different now
more distinct
as through new glasses.
And the sky
was it ever so blue?

And all the time
deepdown in the deserted busshelter of his mind
he thinks about his journey nearly done.
One day he'll clock on and never clock off
or clock off and never clock on.

What the Littlegirl Did

The littlegirl
   pulled up her bellyskin
      like a vest
         and examined her chest
            spleen, kidneys and the rest
               as a measled child a rash.

Sugar and spice
   and everything nice
      that's what littlegirls are made of

So she put in a hand
   and pulled out a gland
      and said: 'What a strange girl am I'

Goodbat Nightman

God bless all policemen
and fighters of crime,
May thieves go to jail
for a very long time.

They've had a hard day
helping clean up the town,
Now they hang from the mantelpiece
both upside down.

A glass of warm blood
and then straight up the stairs,
Batman and Robin
are saying their prayers.

. . . . . .

They've locked all the doors
and they've put out the bat,
Put on their batjamas
(They like doing that)

They've filled their batwater-bottles
made their batbeds,
With two springy battresses
for sleepy batheads.

They're closing red eyes
and they're counting black sheep,
Batman and Robin
are falling asleep.

What You Are

you are the cat's paw
among the silence of midnight goldfish

you are the waves
which cover my feet like cold eiderdowns

you are the teddybear (as good as new)
found beside a road accident

you are the lost day
in the life of a child murderer

you are the underwatertree
around which fish swirl like leaves

you are the green
whose depths I cannot fathom

you are the clean sword
that slaughtered the first innocent

you are the blind mirror
before the curtains are drawn back

you are the drop of dew on a petal
before the clouds weep blood

you are the sweetfresh grass that goes sour
and rots beneath children's feet

you are the rubber glove
dreading the surgeon's brutal hand

you are the wind caught on barbedwire
and crying out against war

you are the moth
entangled in a crown of thorns

you are the apple for teacher
left in a damp cloakroom

you are the smallpox injection
glowing on the torchsinger's arm like a swastika

you are the litmus leaves
quivering on the suntan trees

you are the ivy
which muffles my walls

you are the first footprints in the sand
on bankholiday morning

you are the suitcase full of limbs
waiting in a leftluggage office
to be collected like an orphan

you are the musical queen
atattention
in a smokefilled deserted cinema

you are a derelict canal
where the tincans whistle no tunes

you are the virgin's bottom drawer
full of pillowslips and crisp loins

you are the bleakness of winter before the cuckoo
catching its feathers on a thornbush
heralded spring

you are the stillness of Van Gogh
before he painted the yellow vortex of his last sun

you are the still grandeur of the Lusitania
before she tripped over the torpedo
and laid a world war of american dead
at the foot of the blarneystone

you are the distance
between Hiroshima and Calvary
measured in mother's kisses

you are the distance
between the accident and the telephone box
measured in heartbeats

you are the distance
between power and politicians
measured in half-masts

you are the distance
between advertising and neuroses
measured in phallic symbols

you are the distance
between you and me
measured in tears

you are the moment
before the noose clenched its fist
and the innocent man cried: treason

you are the moment
before the warbooks in the public library
turned into frogs and croaked khaki obscenities

you are the moment
before the buildings turned into flesh
and windows closed their eyes

you are the moment
before the railwaystations burst into tears
and the bookstalls picked their noses

you are the moment
before the buspeople turned into teeth
and chewed the inspector
for no other reason than he was doing his duty

you are the moment
before the flowers turned into plastic and melted
in the heat of the burning cities

you are the moment
before the blindman puts on his dark glasses

you are the moment
before the subconscious begged to be left in peace

you are the moment
before the world was made flesh

you are the moment
before the clouds became locomotives
and hurtled headlong into the sun

you are the moment
before the television personality took off his trousers
and said: see I am just a man

you are the moment
before the spotlight moving across the darkened stage
like a crab finds the singer

you are the moment
before the seed nestles in the womb

you are the moment
before the clocks had nervous breakdowns
and refused to keep pace with man's madness

you are the moment
before the cattle were herded together like men

you are the moment
before God forgot His lines

you are the moment
before we learned that the maninthemoon was queer
and some of us fled into the forests

you are the moment of pride
before the fiftieth bead

you are the moment
before the poem passed peacefully away at dawn
like a monarch

There's Something Sad

There's something sad
about the glass
with lipstick on its mouth
that's pointed at and given back
to the waitress in disgust

    Like the girl with the hair-lip
        whom
            no one
                wants
                    to
                        kiss.

Vinegar

sometimes
i feel like a priest
in a fish & chip queue
quietly thinking
as the vinegar runs through
how nice it would be
to buy supper for two

M. 66

The politicians,
(who are buying huge cars with hobnailed
    wheels the size of merry-go-rounds)
        have a new plan.
        They are going to
        put cobbles
        in our eyesockets
        and pebbles
        in our navels
        and fill us up
        with asphalt
        and lay us
        side by side
so that we can take a more active part
        in the road
        to destruction.

The Fish

you always were a strange girl now weren't you?
like the midsummernights party we went to
where towards witching
being tired and hot of dancing
we slipped thro' the frenchwindows
and arminarmed across the lawn

pausing at the artificial pond
lying liquidblack and limped
in the stricttempo air we kissed
when suddenly you began to tremble
and removing one lavender satin glove knelt
and slipped your hand into the slimy mirror

your face was sad as you brought forth
a switching twitching silver fish
which you lay at my feet
and as the quick tick of the grass
gave way to the slow flop of death
stillkneeling you said softly: 'dont die little fish'

then you tookoff your other glove
and we lay sadly and we made love
as the dancers danced slowly
the fish stared coldly
and the moon admired its reflection
in the lilypetalled pond

Dreampoem

in a corner of my bedroom
    grew a tree
    a happytree
    my own tree
its leaves were soft
    like flesh
and its birds sang poems for me
then
    without warning
two men
    with understanding smiles
and axes
    made out of forged excuses
came and chopped it down
either   yesterday
    or the day before
i think it was the day before

Mother the Wardrobe is Full of Infantrymen

mother the wardrobe is full of infantrymen
i did i asked them
but they snarled saying it was a mans life

mother there is a centurian tank in the parlour
i did i asked the officer
but he laughed saying 'Queens regulations'
(piano was out of tune anyway)

mother polish your identity bracelet
there is a mushroom cloud in the backgarden
i did i tried to bring in the cat
but it simply came to pieces in my hand
i did i tried to whitewash the windows
but there weren't any
i did i tried to hide under the stairs
but i couldn't get in for civil defence leaders
i did i tried ringing candid camera
but they crossed their hearts

i went for a policeman but they were looting the town
i went out for a fire engine but they were all upside down
i went for a priest but they were all on their knees
mother don't just lie there say something please
mother don't just lie there say something please

A Square Dance

In Flanders fields in Northern France
They're all doing a brand new dance
It makes you happy and out of breath
And it's called the Dance of Death

Everybody stands in line
Everybody's feeling fine
We're all going to a hop
1 – 2 – 3 and over the top

It's the dance designed to thrill
It's the mustard gas quadrille
A dance for men – girls have no say in it
For your partner is a bayonet

See how the dancers sway and run
To the rhythm of the gun
Swing your partner dos-y-doed
All around the shells explode

Honour your partner form a square
Smell the burning in the air
Over the barbed wire kicking high
Men like shirts hung out to dry

Everybody claps his hand
To the swinging German Band
When you're tired hold your head
Stumble, fall, pretend you're dead

When you're ready for some fun
Up you get and kill a hun
In khaki evening dress you're grand
The Victor Sylvester of no man's land

In Flanders fields where mortars blaze
They're all doing the latest craze
Khaki dancers out of breath
Doing the glorious Dance of Death
Doing the glorious (*clap, clap*) Dance of Death.

Let Me Die a Youngman's Death

Let me die a youngman's death
not a clean & inbetween
the sheets holywater death
not a famous-last-words
peaceful out of breath death

When I'm 73
& in constant good tumour
may I be mown down at dawn
by a bright red sports car
on my way home
from an allnight party

Or when I'm 91
with silver hair
& sitting in a barber's chair
may rival gangsters
with hamfisted tommyguns burst in
& give me a short back & insides

Or when I'm 104
& banned from the Cavern
may my mistress
catching me in bed with her daughter
& fearing her son
cut me up into little pieces
& throw away every piece but one

Let me die a youngman's death
not a free from sin tiptoe in
candle wax & waning death
not a curtains drawn by angels borne
'what a nice way to go' death

BRIAN PATTEN

Party Piece

He said:
'Let's stay here
Now this place has emptied
& make gentle pornography with one another,
While the partygoers go out
& the dawn creeps in,
Like a stranger.

Let us not hesitate
Over what we know
Or over how cold this place has become,
But let's unclip our minds
And let tumble free
The mad, mangled crocodiles of love.'

So they did,
Right there among the woodbines and guinness stains,
And later he caught a bus and she a train
And all there was between them then
was rain.

Little Johnny's Confession

This morning
    being rather young and foolish
    I borrowed a machinegun my father
    had left hidden since the war, went out,
    and eliminated a number of small enemies.
    Since then I have not returned home.

This morning
    swarms of police with trackerdogs
    wander about the city
    with my description printed
    on their minds, asking:
    'Have you seen him,
    He is seven years old,
    likes Pluto, Mighty Mouse
    and Biffo The Bear,
    have you seen him, anywhere?'

This morning
    sitting alone in a strange playground,
    muttering Youve blundered Youve blundered
    over and over to myself
    I work out my next move
    but cannot move;
    the trackerdogs will sniff me out,
    they have my lollypops.

Where Are You Now, Batman?

Where are you now, Batman? Now that Aunt Heriot has
      reported Robin missing
And Superman's fallen asleep in the sixpenny childhood
      seats?
Where are you now that Captain Marvel's SHAZAM!
      echoes round the auditorium,
The magicians don't hear it,
Must all be deaf ... or dead ...
The Purple Monster who came down from the Purple
      Planet disguised as a man
Is wandering aimlessly about the streets
With no way of getting back.
Sir Galahad's been strangled by the Incredible Living
      Trees,
Zorro killed by his own sword.
Blackhawk has buried the last of his companions
And has now gone off to commit suicide in the disused
      Hangars of Innocence.
The Monster and the Ape still fight it out in a room
Where the walls are continually closing in;
Rocketman's fuel tanks gave out over London.
Even Flash Gordon's lost, he wanders among the stars
Weeping over the woman he loved
7 Universes ago.
      My celluloid companions, it's only a few
          years
Since I knew you. Something in us has faded.
      Has the Terrible Fiend, That Ghastly
          Adversary,
Mr Old Age, Caught you in his deadly trap,
And come finally to polish you off,
His machinegun dripping with years ...?

A Green Sportscar

for Mal Doft, racedriver

... And later, to come across
those couples in gleaming green sportscars,
riveted with steel and sprinkled with dawn;
and still shaking in tarpaulin hoods, the rain
spills onto their faces
as the daylight exposes their E-type deaths.

... And later still, to discover
inside him, something has been moved.
She stretched out across him, breasts
pointing towards dawn, who found her last kick
in the sound of the skid on tarmac
of the green-steel coffin in its quiet field.

... And finally, to understand them;
they who having been switched off permanently,
are so very still. You would think them asleep,
not dead, if not for the evidence, their expressions
caught at dawn, and held tight beneath
this accidental incident.

After Breakfast

After breakfast,
Which is usually coffee and a view
Of teeming rain and the Cathedral old and grey but
Smelling good with grass and ferns
I go out thinking of all those people who've come into this
room

And have slept here
Sad and naked
Alone in pairs
Who came together and
Were they young and white with
Some hint of innocence?
Or did they come simply to come,
To fumble then finally tumble apart,
Or, were they older still, past sex,
Lost in mirrors, contemplating their decay and
What did the morning mean to them?

Perhaps once this room was the servants quarter.
Was she young with freckles, with apple breasts?
Did she ever laugh?
Tease the manservant with her 19th Century charms
And her skirts whirling,
Did she look out through the skylight
And wish she were free, and
What did she have for breakfast?

Waking this morning I think
How good it would be to have someone to share breakfast
with.

Whole families waking!
A thousand negligees, pyjamas, nightgowns
All wandering down to breakfast

How secure! and
Others coming out the far end of dawn
Having only pain and drizzle for breakfast,
Waking always to be greeted with the poor feast of daylight.

How many halflives
Sulking behind these windows
From basement to attic
Complaining and asking
Who will inherit me today?
Who will I share breakfast with?
And always the same answer coming back –

The rain will inherit you – lonely breakfaster!

Sing Softly

Sing softly
now sadly
of rains he has known,

of dawns when
his visions
were of damp boys

slim and brown,
walking at the edge
of cold rivers.

O they were
the palest of children,
stripping.

Slim fish
darting through water,
laughing now and then.

Seascape

gulls kiss the sun
and you walk on the beach
afraid of the tide

from the sea's warm belly
a lobster crawls to
see if we've gone

but mouths still talk
and finding out my lips
I say to you:

'lie silently
and stretch out your arms
like seaweed strangled by the wind'

out of a seashell
a sandcrab pokes his head
and sniffs the salt wind

now afraid we sit in silence
and watching the sun go down
I ask you your name

Somewhere Between Heaven and Woolworths,
A Song

She keeps kingfishers in their cages
And goldfish in their bowls,
She is lovely and is afraid
Of such things as growing cold.

There were numerous men that loved her,
Though they were more cruel than kind
And their love an act in isolation,
A form of pantomime.

She says she has now forgotten
The feelings that she shared
At various all-night parties
Among the couples on the stairs,

For among the songs and the dancing
She was once open wide,
A girl dressed in denim
With the boys dressed in lies.

She's eating roses on toast with tulip butter;
Praying for her mirror to stay young;
Though on its no longer gilted surface
This message she has scrawled:

'O somewhere between Heaven and Woolworths
I live I love I scold,
I keep kingfishers in their cages
And goldfish in their bowls.'

I'm Dreaming of a White Smethwick

An old, never-to-be-forgotten song

I'm dreaming of a white Smethwick,
One I didn't want to know,
Where they'll have allwhite, allright children
And the White and White Minstrel Show.

I'm dreaming of a white Smethwick
Where they'll have a brandnew dance;
Teach their kids to close their eyes
And forget that once

Strange men came to Smethwick
With slogans whitewashed on their minds,
They campaigned about a while
And left their shit behind.

I saw black father christmasses
Burning in the snow,
Protesting to the Opposition
About what happened a while ago.

The last blackbird's been shot in Smethwick
And the council's doing allright,
The M.P.'s in the Commons
Making sure his words are white.

Chorus: May all your days be merry and bright
        And may all your citizens be white.

NOTE: As in numerous folk songs, the words may be improvised on
to suit the present.

Sleep Now

In Memory of Wilfred Owen

Sleep now,
Your blood moving in the quiet wind;
No longer afraid of the rabbits
Hurrying through the tall grass
Or the faces laughing on the beach
And among the cold trees.

Sleep now,
Alone in the sleeves of grief,
Listening to clothes falling
And to your flesh touching God;
To the chatter and backslapping
Of Christ meeting heroes of war.

Sleep now,
Your words have passed
The lights shining from the East
And the sound of the flack
Raping graves and emptying seasons.

You do not hear the dry wind pray
Or the children play
A game called 'Soldiers' in the street.

Song for Last Year's Wife

Alice, this is my first winter
of waking without you, of knowing
that you, dressed in familiar clothes
are elsewhere, perhaps not even
conscious of our anniversary. Have
you noticed? The earth's still as hard,
the same empty gardens exist; it is
as if nothing special had changed.
I wake with another mouth feeding
from me, yet still feel as if
Love had not the right
to walk out of me. A year now. So
what? you say. I send out my spies
to discover what you are doing. They smile,
return, tell me your body's as firm,
you are as alive, as warm and inviting
as when I knew you first. . . . Perhaps it is
the winter, its isolation from other seasons,
that sends me your ghost to witness
when I wake. Somebody came here today, asked
how you were keeping, what
you were doing. I imagine you,
waking in another city, touched
by this same hour. So ordinary
a thing as loss comes now and touches me.

Prosepoem Towards a Definition of Itself

When in public poetry should take off its clothes and wave to the nearest person in sight; it should be seen in the company of thieves and lovers rather than that of journalists and publishers. On sighting mathematicians it should unhook the algebra from their minds and replace it with poetry; on sighting poets it should unhook poetry from their minds and replace it with algebra; it should fall in love with children and woo them with fairytales; it should wait on the landing for 2 years for its mates to come home then go outside and find them all dead.

When the electricity fails it should wear dark glasses and pretend to be blind. It should guide all those who are safe into the middle of busy roads and leave them there. It should scatter woodworm into the bedrooms of all peg-legged men not being afraid to hurt the innocent or make such differences. It should shout EVIL! EVIL! from the roofs of the world's stock exchanges. It should not pretend to be a clerk or a librarian. It should be kind, it is the eventual sameness of contradictions. It should never weep until it is alone and then only after it has covered the mirrors and sealed up the cracks.

Poetry should seek out pale and lyrical couples and wander with them into stables, neglected bedrooms and engineless cars for a final Good Time. It should enter burning factories too late to save anyone. It should pay no attention to its real name.
Poetry should be seen lying by the side of road accidents, hissing from unlit gassrings. It should scrawl the nymphomaniac's secret on her teacher's blackboard; offer her a worm saying: Inside this is a tiny apple. Poetry should play hopscotch in the 6pm streets and look for jinks in other

people's dustbins. At dawn it should leave the bedroom and catch the first bus home to its wife. At dusk it should chatup a girl nobody wants. It should be seen standing on the ledge of a skyscraper, on a bridge with a brick tied around its heart. It is the monster hiding in a child's dark room, it is the scar on a beautiful man's face. It is the last blade of grass being picked from the city park.

Maud, 1965

Maud, where are you Maud?
With your long dresses and peachcream complexion;
In what cage did you hang that black bat night?
What took place in the garden? Maud, it is over,
You can tell us now.

Still lyrical but much used, you wander about the suburbs
Watching the buses go past full of young happy people,
Wondering where the garden is, wherever can it be,
And how can it be lost. Maud, it's no use.

Can it be that you got yourself lost
And are living with an out of work musician,
You share a furnished room and have an old wireless
That tells you the latest bad news.
What's happening Maud?

Do you wear a Mary Quant dress
And eat fish and chips alone at night?
Where are you? and are you very lost,
Very much alone? Do you have stupendous dreams
And wake with one hand on your breast, and
The other on your cunt?
Do you cry for that garden, lost among pornographic
    suggestions,
Where the concrete flowers neither open nor close;
Who poured weedkiller over your innocence?

We could not find that garden for you,
Even if we tried.
So, come into the city Maud,
Where the flowers are too quickly picked
And the days are murdered as if they were enemies.

Maud, is that you I see
Alone among the office blocks,
Head bowed, young tears singing pop-sorrow
On your cheeks?

The River Arse

The rain is teeming
    across the river
falling on the arse of
    a nude girl swimming
without even a splash
    & O it's such a pretty little arse.
see how it rises now and then
    like an island
a pink island moving through the water
    something young and good
in the river that flows out of Lyons
    a nude arse and a special one at that
belonging to a swimmer floating
    in the opposite direction
to the shore.

Room

Room you're toneless now.
Room you don't belong to me
I want another room I want one
without your tattymemories
I want to brush you out into the streets where
you'll become a debris full of children's laughter
Room you're murderous
You're a crooked woman with armpits full of lice
You're no good to me
You make me feel like an accident
Make me blush with your crude jokes
and your old iron bedsteads
Room you've made me weep too many times
I'm sick of you and all your faces
I go into houses and find its still you only this time
you're wearing a different disguise
I send out my spies to find who you're living with
but they don't return
I send myself out and find you eating my spies.
Its impossible. You stand there dusty and naked
Your records spinning mutely
Your bed throwing gleeming girlbodies at the armies
of wage clerks who prance in you
Your books all empty
Your gasstoves hissing
Wallpaper crying sighing it doesn't matter
for your windows have become taperecordings of the night
and only death will shove you to sleep.
I'm going to leave you
Going to spend all my dreams
Once in you I could lie and hear the spyingmoon apologize
as it tiptoed through the clouds
and left you in your special darkness

But its different now, now
only the rain splatters through
and the one other sound is you whispering
'I'm not around you I'm in you all my walls are in you'
Room you're full of my own graves!

A Creature to Tell the Time By

I created for myself
a creature to tell the time by
   – & on the lawns of her tongue
flowers grew,
    sweet scented words fell
out her mouth,
her eyes and paws as well were comforting –
    & woken with her
    at dawn, with living birds
humming, alien
inside my head,
I noticed inside us both
the green love that grew there yesterday
    was dead.

Schoolboy

Before playtime let us consider the possibilities
of getting stoned on milk.

    In his dreams,
scribbling overcharged on woodbines,
mumbling obscure sentences into his desk
'No way of getting out,
no way out ...'
                Poet dying of
too much education, schoolfriends, examinations,
canes that walk the nurseries of his wet dreams;
satchels full of chewing gum, bad jokes, pencils;
crude drawings performed in the name of art. Soon will
come the Joyful Realization in Mary's back kitchen
       while mother's out.
All this during chemistry.

(The headmaster's crying in his study.
His old pinstriped pants rolled up to his knees
in a vain attempt to recapture youth; emotions
skid along his slippery age; Love, smeared across his face,
like a road accident.)

The schoolyard's full of people to hate.
Full of tick and prefects and a fat schoolmaster
and whistles and older and younger boys, but
he's growing
  sadly
    growing
      up.

Girls,
  becoming mysterious, are now more important
than arriving at school late or receiving trivial awards.

Postcards of those huge women
                seem a little more believable now.

(Secretly, the pale, unmarried headmaster telling him
Death is the only grammatically correct full-
                                                stop.)

Girls,
    still mysterious;
arithmetic thighed, breasts measured in thumbprints,
not inches.
Literature's just another way out.
History's full of absurd mistakes.
King Arthur if he ever existed
would only have farted and excused himself
from the Round Table in a hurry.

(The headmaster, staring through the study window
into the playground, composes evil poems about
the lyrical boy in class four)
                'He invited us up sir,
                    but not for the cane,
                        said the algebra of life
                            was too difficult to explain
                            and that all equations
                                mounted to nothing....'

Growing up's wonderful if
                you keep your eyes
                    closed tightly, and
if you manage to grow
            take your soul with you,
                nobody wants it.

So,
playtime's finished with;
it's time to pull the last sad chain
                on his last
            sadschoolgirlcrush.

It is time to fathom out too many things.
To learn he's no longer got somebody watching over him;
he's going to know strange things, learn
how to lie correctly, how to lay correctly,
how to cheat and steal in the nicest possible manner.
He will learn amongst other things, how to enjoy
his enemies, and how to avoid friendships. If he's unlucky
he will learn how to love and give everything away
and how eventually, he'll end up with nothing.

        He won't understand many things.
He'll just accept them. He'll experiment with hardboiled
            eggs all his life
and die a stranger in a race attempting Humanity.

    And finally,
the playground full of dust,
    crates of sour milk lining the corridors;
        the headmaster, weeping quietly among the saws and
                                    chisels
            in the damp woodwork room;

        The ghosts of Tim and Maureen and Pat
            and Nancy and so many others,
        all holding sexless hands, all
                doomed to living, and
one pale boy
in a steamy room

looking outside across the roofs and chimneys
where it seems, the clouds are crying,
the daylight's gone blind
and his teachers, all dead.

Delicate John

Delicate John has moved away.
Listen to what the children said:

He couldn't make love
And he couldn't make money,
He had a gammy leg
(which they thought was funny).

Now John, tender and quiet as a habit,
is leading half a life among his books.
He cannot return from where he came
Because the children learnt

Of what they thought a lack of love,
Of his lack of money,
Of something unfamiliar in his brain
(which they thought was funny)

He sits at a window and sometimes they pass,
The children who gave him a monkey for his back,
They pass in twos they pass in threes,
They look contented and they look pleased.
John sits, he rots away,
Behind a lace curtain where he quietly cries
Tears as big as a choir boy's eyes.

What have they done to John,
What have they done to him?
The children who grow old,
Who squabble and grow thin,
Who lick their lips at disaster
And quietly whisper of sin.

On a Horse Called Autumn

(For Maureen)

On a horse called autumn
among certain decaying things
she rides inside me, for

no matter where I move
this puzzled woman sings
of nude horsemen, breeched
in leather,

of stables decaying near
where once
riders came,

and where now alone
her heart journeys, among
lies I made real.

Now riding in truth
what alterations can I make
knowing nothing will change?

Things stay the same:
such journeys as hers
are the ones I care for.

A Talk with a Wood

Moving through you one evening
when you offered shelter to
quiet things soaked in rain

I saw through your thinning branches
the beginnings of suburbs, and
frightened by the rain,

grey hares running upright in
distant fields; and quite alone there
I thought of nothing but my footprints

being filled, and love, distilled
of people, drifted free, then
the woods spoke with me.

Travelling Between Places

Leaving nothing and nothing ahead;
when you stop for the evening
the sky will be in ruins,

when you hear late birds
with tired throats singing
think how good it is that they,

knowing you were coming,
stayed up late to greet you
who travels between places

when the late afternoon
drifts into the woods, when
nothing matters specially.

The Fruitful Lady of Dawn

She walks across the room and opens the skylight
thinking, perhaps a bird will drop in
and teach me how to sing.

She attempts to understand why a sentence made of kisses
is followed by the image
of somebody wandering alone through semi-colons

but cannot fathom out
whose dawn she belongs in,
so among them is silent

and under the skylight
puts on a red dress calling it a blue one;
she approaches breakfast as she would a lover,

she is alive!
and one of her body's commonest needs
I have made holy

For she will feed my pink bird
She will make love in technicolour
She will be the fruitful lady of dawn.

In a New Kind of Dawn

In a new kind of dawn
readjusting your conscience
you wake, and

woken you dream
or so it seems
of forests you've come across

& lives you'd have swum in
had you been strong enough.

On the Dawn Boat

on the dawn boat,
coming awake,
the land empty, I thought

about it, about
the many warnings,
the many signs, but

none to lead me
away from here, none
to lead me there.

Looking Back at It

At nineteen I was a brave Old Hunchback
    Climbing to 'tremendous heights'
Preparing to swing down on my golden rope
    And rescue the Accused Innocence.
But on my swooping, downwards path one day
          Innocence ducked
And I amazed at such an act crashed into
    A wall she had been building,

How silly now to think myself able to rescue anything!

The Beast

Something that was not there before
has come through the mirror
into my room.

It is not such a simple creature
as at first I thought –
from somewhere it has brought a mischief

that troubles both silence and objects
and now left alone here
I weave intricate reasons for its arrival.

They disintegrate. Today in January, with
the light frozen on my window, I hear outside
a million panicking birds, and know even out there

comfort is done with; it has shattered
even the stars, this creature
at last come home to me.

MORE ABOUT PENGUINS

Penguinews, which appears every month, contains details of all the new books issued by Penguins as they are published. From time to time it is supplemented by *Penguins in Print,* which is a complete list of all books published by Penguins which are in print. (There are well over three thousand of these.)

A specimen copy of *Penguinews* will be sent to you free on request, and you can become a subscriber for the price of the postage – 30p for a year's issues (including the complete lists) if you live in the United Kingdom, or 60p if you live elsewhere. Just write to Dept EP, Penguin Books Ltd, Harmondsworth, Middlesex, enclosing a cheque or postal order, and your name will be added to the mailing list.

Other volumes in Penguin Modern Poets are listed overleaf.

Note: *Penguinews* and *Penguins in Print*
are not available in the U.S.A. or Canada

*NOT FOR SALE IN THE U.S.A.
†NOT FOR SALE IN THE U.S.A. OR CANADA